Ancient Egypt was ruled by a king called a
pharaoh. He lived in a palace in a big city.
Hundreds of officials carried out his orders.
Writers, called scribes, kept records of crops
and collected taxes. Potters, weavers and other
craftsmen made everyday things people needed.
The poorest people were farmers and labourers.

3

A river boat

River boats were made from papyrus reeds lashed together in long bundles.

You will need:

Corrugated card	Pencil	Scissors
PVA glue	Paints	Paintbrush

Follow the steps . . .

1. Cut a strip of corrugated card into the shape of a long leaf like this.

2. Cut four more strips the same size. Glue the strips one on top of the other.

3. While the glue is wet, bend up the ends of the strips to make a boat shape.

4. Paint your boat when the glue has dried.

THE Egyptians

Ruth Thomson

Contents

3000 BC	2000 BC	1000 BC	0	1000 AD	2000 AD

Egyptians

Greeks

Romans

Vikings

W
FRANKLIN WATTS
LONDON•SYDNEY

Who were the Egyptians?

The Egyptians lived beside the River Nile. Most of Egypt was sandy, rocky desert. Every year, the Nile flooded the land on either side of it. When the water went down, it left behind a layer of thick, black soil. This was perfect for growing crops, so people always had food.

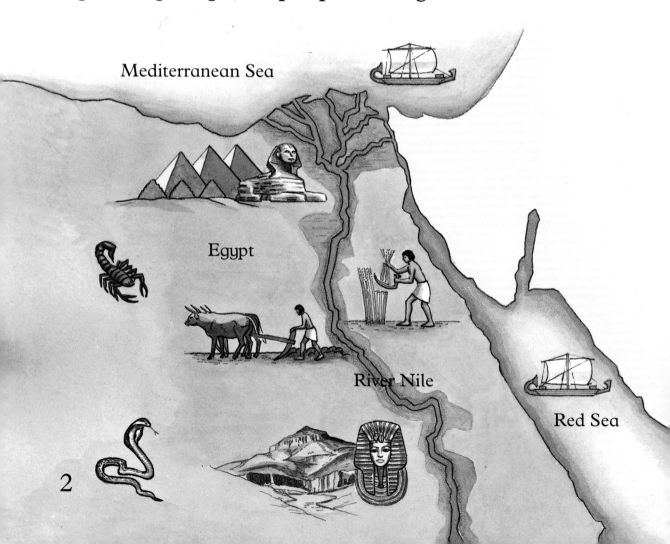

Mediterranean Sea

Egypt

River Nile

Red Sea

2

A collar necklace

You will need:

Saucepan lid	Pencil	Card
Scissors	Saucer	Paints

Follow the steps . . .

1. Draw around a large saucepan lid on to a piece of white card. Cut it out.

2. Put a saucer in the middle and draw around it to make a smaller circle.

   Cut

3. Cut a wedge from the outer circle to the inner one. Cut out the inner circle. Try on your collar. Cut a bigger hole if it does not fit you.

4. Fingerpaint the collar with bright paints to look like jewels.

Homes

All houses were built of mud-and-straw bricks,
baked hard in the sun. Their thick walls and
small windows kept out the heat of the sun.
The houses of rich people had many rooms with
wall paintings and tiled floors. They also had
large gardens with pools.

However, most houses had only a few rooms, with whitewashed walls and an earth floor. People had very little furniture. They slept on wooden beds and sat on stools or cushions. People often cooked and slept under a cloth canopy on the flat roof.

A model house

You will need:

Modelling tools   Clay   Board   Knife

Follow the steps . . .

1. Flatten some clay on the board.
   Cut it into an oval for a courtyard.

2. Put a big lump of clay on one end
   of the courtyard. Shape it into a house.
   Carve some steps and hollow
   out the inside.

3. Roll and cut out a flat wall.
   Join it to the front of the house.
   Cut out a window.
   Add an arched door.

4. Put a low wall all around the courtyard.

A painted chest

The ancient Egyptians kept their clothes in chests or boxes. Food was stored in clay jars.

You will need:

Shoe box with lid	Pencil	Scissors
Card	Paints and brush	Glue

Follow the steps . . .

1. Paint the box and the lid all over.

2. Cut out four pieces of card for legs. Roll them into tubes and glue them. Paint them and let them dry.

3. Snip into the ends of the legs. Open them out. Glue one leg to each corner of the box.

4. Cut four small circles of card. Glue one to the other end of each leg.

The pharaoh

The pharaoh was the ruler of Egypt. The people believed he was a god on earth and that he had the powers of a god.

The pharaoh was the head of the government, the army and the law courts. He was the chief priest of the temples. He owned all the granaries where food was stored.

Thousands of officials carried out the pharaoh's orders. The most important official was called the *vizier*. Wealthy nobles were in charge of the water supply, the granaries and tax collecting. The Egyptians did not use money. People paid taxes with crops or other goods, or they worked on the pharaoh's building projects.

Writing with pictures

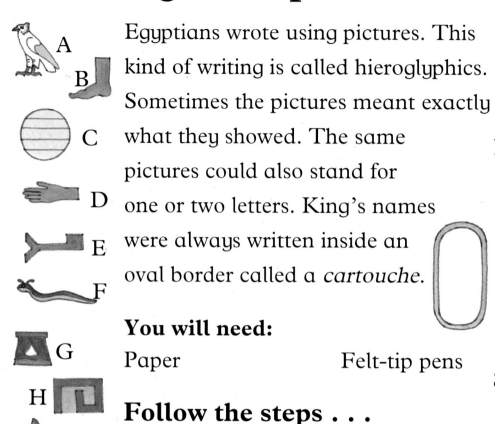

Egyptians wrote using pictures. This kind of writing is called hieroglyphics. Sometimes the pictures meant exactly what they showed. The same pictures could also stand for one or two letters. King's names were always written inside an oval border called a *cartouche*.

You will need:

Paper   Felt-tip pens

Follow the steps . . .

1. Write some hieroglyphs.

2. Can you read the name in the photograph?

3. Use the hieroglyphs to write your name inside a *cartouche*.

17

The pyramids

Some of the first pharaohs had enormous tombs, called pyramids, built for them. They were built from stone blocks. Some are still standing today.

The Egyptians believed that when people died they went to a new world. They filled tombs with clothes, food, furniture, jewels and clay figures of servants. They thought the dead people would need these things to make their new life comfortable.

Artists painted scenes on the inside of the tomb. These showed the life people hoped to have in their new world after death.

The pharaohs' pyramids held such great treasures that robbers tried to steal from them. Later pharaohs built tombs underground with maze-like corridors to secret burial chambers.

A mummy

The Egyptians believed a dead person would need his body in another life. To keep it from rotting in the tomb, they took out the insides, dried the body and wrapped it in linen bandages. The body was then called a mummy.

You will need:

Cardboard tube	Scissors	Newspaper	PVA glue
Sticky tape	Stone	Card	Paint

Follow the steps . . .

1. Push a ball of newspaper into one end of the tube. Tape on folded strips of newspaper for the arms.

2. Put a stone in the other end of the cylinder. Tape a card rectangle over it. Add feet made from newspaper.

3. Cover the mummy with newspaper strips dipped in glue. Leave it to dry. Paint it.

A scarab amulet

An amulet was a charm which the Egyptians believed would protect them against evil. Amulets were worn, or buried with mummies, to ward off evil spirits. The scarab (beetle) was the symbol of the most important Egyptian god – the sun god.

You will need:

Modelling clay   Modelling tool or blunt pencil

Follow the steps . . .

1. Shape the clay into an oval dome shape.

2. Model the shape of the head and the body.

3. Carve a pattern on the scarab's back using the modelling tool or a blunt pencil.

INDEX

Entries in *italics* are activity pages.

© 1995 Franklin Watts
This edition 2001

Franklin Watts
96 Leonard Street
London EC2A 4XD

Franklin Watts Australia
56 O'Riordan Street
Alexandria, Sydney
NSW 2015

ISBN 0 7496 4169 X

Dewey Decimal Classification
Number 932

A CIP catalogue record for this
book is available from the British
Library.

10 9 8 7 6 5 4

Editor: Annabel Martin
Consultant: Richard Tames
Design: Mike Davis
Artwork: Cilla Eurich
          Ruth Levy
Photographs: Peter Millard

Printed in Malaysia